What is a bird?

by Feana Tu'akoi
designed by Vasanti Unka

SCHOLASTIC
AUCKLAND SYDNEY NEW YORK LONDON TORONTO
MEXICO CITY NEW DELHI HONG KONG

for Sione

Published in 2007 by Scholastic New Zealand Limited
Private Bag 94407, Greenmount, Manukau 2141, New Zealand

Scholastic Australia Pty Limited
PO Box 579, Gosford, NSW 2250, Australia

Text © Feana Tu'akoi, 2007

ISBN 978-1-86943-803-6

All rights reserved. No part of this publication may be reproduced or transmitted in any form or by any means, electronic, mechanical or digital, including photocopying, recording, storage in any information retrieval system, or otherwise, without prior written permission of the publisher.

National Library of New Zealand Cataloguing-in-Publication Data

Tu'akoi, Feana.
What is a bird? / by Feana Tu'akoi.
(What is a)
ISBN 978-1-86943-803-6
1. Birds—Juvenile literature. [1. Birds.] I. Title. II. Series: Tu'akoi, Feana. What is a.
598—dc 22

9 8 7 6 5 4 3 2   7 8 9 / 0

Publishing team: Christine Dale, Penny Scown and Annette Bisman
Design: Vasanti Unka
Photographic research: Penny Scown
Typeset in 17/22pt ITC Stone Informal

Every effort has been made to trace copyright holders of material used in this book. If any rights have been omitted the publisher offers sincere apologies and will rectify this matter in any subsequent reprint, following notification.

Photos from Wikipedia are either in the Public Domain or have been reproduced under the GNU Free Documentation Licence agreement, or Creative Commons.

What is a bird?

Let's see …

If it flies, it is a bird.

Not always ...

Most birds **do** fly, but some birds don't.

Ostriches, emus and penguins are birds, but they don't fly.

Some things that fly are not birds.

Bats fly and so do some insects.
But bats and insects are not birds.

If it has wings, it is a bird.

Not always ...

Birds **do** have wings,
but so do bats and some insects.

Some birds, like kiwi,
have tiny wings that
you cannot see very well.
Penguins have wings they use for swimming.

If it lays eggs, it is a bird.

Not always ...

Female birds **do** lay eggs, but so do other creatures.

Most female reptiles lay eggs.

Fish, flies and spiders lay eggs, too.
But reptiles, fish, flies and spiders are not birds.

If it makes a nest, it is a bird.

Not always ...

Most birds **do** make nests, but not all birds.

Cuckoos don't make nests. They lay their eggs in other birds' nests.

Mice, wasps, bees and some snakes make nests, but they are not birds.

If it sings, it is a bird.

Not always ...

Some birds **do** sing, but not all birds.
Vultures are birds,
but they do not sing.

Some things that sing are not birds.
Grasshoppers, cicadas, frogs and people sing,
but none of them are birds.

If it has a beak, it is a bird.

Not always …

Birds **do** have beaks,
but not everything that has a beak is a bird.

Dolphins and turtles have beaks, and so do platypuses.
But dolphins, turtles and platypuses are not birds.

If it has no teeth, it is a bird.

Not always …

Birds **don't** have teeth.
But turtles don't have teeth either,
and turtles are not birds.

If it moves on two legs, it is a bird.

Not always ...

Birds **do** move about on two legs, but so do kangaroos, gibbons and people.

And kangaroos, gibbons and people are not birds.

If it has clawed toes, it is a bird.

Not always ...

Birds **do** have clawed toes,
and some birds have sharp,
hooked talons,
which they use to catch prey.

But dogs, otters, squirrels and cats
also have clawed toes, and they are not birds.

If it has feathers, it is a bird.
Yes! Always!

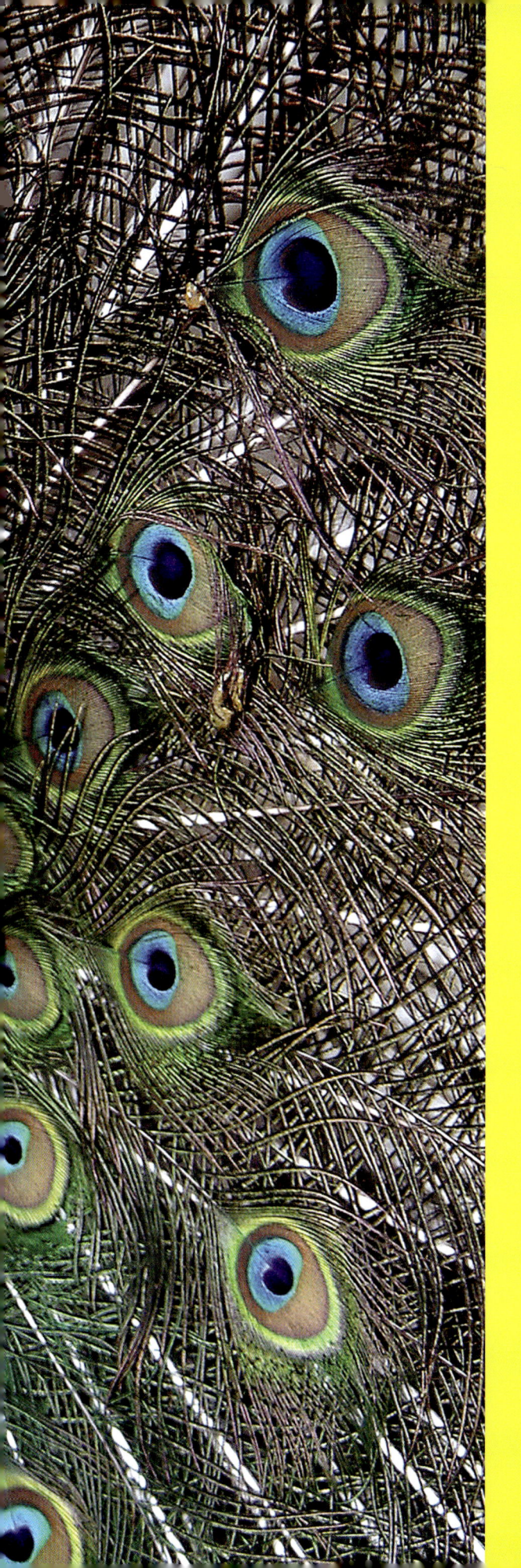

All birds have feathers and they are the only creatures that have them.

If a creature has feathers, it must be a bird.

What is a bird?

There are over 9000 different kinds of birds in the world.

All birds have two wings, but not all birds can fly.
All female birds lay eggs, but they don't all build nests.
Every bird has a beak, two legs, scaly feet and four toes, but no bird has teeth.

Other creatures have some of these characteristics, too.

But only a bird has feathers.

**If it has feathers,
it is a bird.**

23